YOUNG SPO

MIKE
TROUT

SARAH MACHAJEWSKI

PowerKiDS
press.

New York

Published in 2019 by The Rosen Publishing Group, Inc.
29 East 21st Street, New York, NY 10010

First Edition

Editor: Elizabeth Krajnik
Book Design: Michael Flynn

Photo Credits: Cover, pp. 1, 6, 21 Icon Sportswire/Getty Images; cover, pp. 4–23 (background) Eo naya/Shutterstock.com; pp. 5, 9 Jeff Gross/Getty Images Sport/Getty Images; p. 7 G Flume/Getty Images Sport/Getty Images;
p. 8 KonstantinChristian/Shutterstock.com; p. 11 John Williamson/Getty Images Sport/Getty Images; p. 13 © Rich Schultz/AP Images; p. 15 Jonathan Moore/Getty Images Sport/Getty Images; p. 17 Lisa Blumenfeld/Getty Images Sport/Getty Images; p. 18 Ron Vesely/Major League Baseball/Getty Images; p. 19 Mark Cunningham/Getty Images Sport/Getty Images; p. 22 Jamie Squire/Getty Images Sport/Getty Images.

Library of Congress Cataloging-in-Publication Data

Names: Machajewski, Sarah, author.
Title: Mike Trout / Sarah Machajewski.
Description: New York : PowerKids Press, [2019] | Series: Young sports greats
   | Includes index.
Identifiers: LCCN 2018015109| ISBN 9781538330470 (library bound) | ISBN
   9781538330494 (paperback) | ISBN 9781538330500 (6 pack)
Subjects: LCSH: Trout, Mike, 1991–Juvenile literature. | Baseball
   players–United States–Biography–Juvenile literature. | Los Angeles
   Angels (Baseball team)–History–Juvenile literature.
Classification: LCC GV865.T73 M37 2018 | DDC 796.357092 [B] –dc23
LC record available at https://lccn.loc.gov/2018015109

Manufactured in the United States of America

CPSIA Compliance Information: Batch #CS18PK For Further Information contact Rosen Publishing, New York, New York at 1-800-237-9932

CONTENTS

FOR THE LOVE OF THE GAME 4

BORN AN ATHLETE 6

STARTING YOUNG 8

STAR PLAYER 10

MAKING IT TO THE MAJORS 12

GOING PRO 14

ROOKIE OF THE YEAR 16

BETTER AND BETTER 18

ONE OF THE GREATS 20

THE FUTURE IS BRIGHT 22

GLOSSARY 23

INDEX 24

WEBSITES 24

FOR THE LOVE OF THE GAME

Legend has it that Abner Doubleday invented baseball in 1839. No one knows for sure if Doubleday created baseball. However, in the years since its creation, baseball has produced more than its fair share of legends.

Mike Trout is a modern-day **professional** baseball player who has become a legendary player in his own right. A center fielder for the Los Angeles Angels, Trout is seen as one of the most outstanding young players in the history of the game. Through hard work, **dedication**, and talent, Trout has quickly risen to fame.

SPORTS CORNER

In 1845, America's first organized baseball club was formed. The New York Knickerbocker Baseball Club created a set of 20 rules for the game, some of which are still followed today.

TROUT WASN'T ALWAYS A PRO ATHLETE. HE STARTED OUT WITH THE BASICS JUST LIKE ALL OTHER ATHLETES DO. HOWEVER, OVER THE YEARS, HE HAS SHOWN HE HAS SOMETHING SPECIAL OTHER PLAYERS JUST DON'T HAVE.

BORN AN ATHLETE

Michael Nelson Trout was born on August 7, 1991, in Vineland, New Jersey, to Jeff and Debbie Trout. He grew up in Millville, New Jersey, with his parents, his sister, Teal, and his brother, Tyler.

Mike's father Jeff played baseball at the University of Delaware. In 1983, the Minnesota Twins **drafted** him and he played on their minor league team for four years.

DEBBIE TROUT   JEFF TROUT

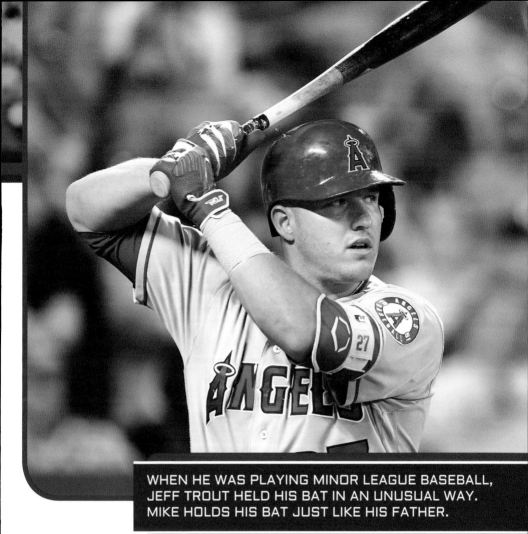

WHEN HE WAS PLAYING MINOR LEAGUE BASEBALL, JEFF TROUT HELD HIS BAT IN AN UNUSUAL WAY. MIKE HOLDS HIS BAT JUST LIKE HIS FATHER.

When Mike Trout was younger, he played Cal Ripken Baseball, which is a division of the Babe Ruth League for four to 12 year olds. His coach said that when Trout was just nine years old, he was one of the best players in his league.

STARTING YOUNG

Many successful baseball players began playing at a young age. Mike Trout is no different. Jeff Trout was a history teacher and football and baseball coach at Millville Senior High School. Jeff said, "I don't think a kid should throw a baseball 365 days a year." He and Debbie wanted to raise Mike to be a good player, but also to listen to his body.

Trout's love of the game stuck with him. He went on to play baseball for Millville Senior High School, where he played the positions of pitcher and shortstop. In his senior year, he played in the outfield.

SPORTS CORNER

Trout also played basketball at Millville High. "I don't think it would matter what he played," his basketball coach, Dale Moore, said. "He has that 'It'."

HIGH SCHOOL WASN'T JUST ABOUT SPORTS FOR MIKE TROUT. HE WAS ALSO A MEMBER OF THE NATIONAL HONOR SOCIETY AND THE LEADERS CLUB.

STAR PLAYER

Trout quickly became Millville's star player. His freshman batting average was .388. By his junior, or third, year, Trout's batting average increased to .530. Throughout his high school **career**, Trout led the Thunderbolts in home runs, runs batted in (RBIs), hits at bat, triples, and bases stolen. He was also a star pitcher.

Trout was named the team captain his junior and senior, or fourth, years. In 2008, the Thunderbolts won their high school conference championship title. While playing for Millville High, Trout also played travel baseball and was invited to try out for the U.S. National squad.

MIKE TROUT POSTED SOME IMPRESSIVE NUMBERS AS A HIGH SCHOOL BASEBALL PLAYER.

TROUT'S HIGH SCHOOL CAREER NUMBERS				
AT BAT	BATTING AVERAGE	RBIs	RUNS	STOLEN BASES
	.436	76	102	51 OF 54
ON THE MOUND	PITCHING RECORD		SHUTOUTS	EARNED RUN AVERAGE (ERA)
	15–4		5	2.22

MAKING IT TO THE MAJORS

By his senior year, Trout was the number-one ranked baseball **prospect** in New Jersey. Nationally, he was ranked number 33 by an organization called Perfect Game. He was a rising talent, and the right people noticed.

In 2009, Trout signed on to play college ball at Eastern Carolina University. But then the majors came calling. In the 2009 MLB draft, the Los Angeles Angels selected Trout as the 25th overall pick. The Angels wanted Trout to be an outfielder even though he had only played that position for one year in high school. Trout's athletic talent was reason enough to pick him.

SPORTS CORNER

Trout is an incredible player. Why was he drafted so low? Great players are usually chosen first in the draft. Some scouts think kids from states that can't play baseball year round are a bigger risk.

EVERY BASEBALL PLAYER DREAMS OF BEING DRAFTED INTO THE MAJOR LEAGUES. FOR MIKE TROUT, HIS DREAM CAME TRUE WHEN HE WAS JUST 19 YEARS OLD.

GOING PRO

After Trout was drafted, he was sent to play for the Angels' minor league team in Arizona. Typically, young players spend several seasons in the minor leagues before they work their way into higher classes of baseball. But Trout isn't a typical player.

Trout was so good that he played a few Class A baseball games in his **rookie** year. The team quickly moved him to Class A Advanced and Double A ball. He put up big numbers, with a batting average of .362. His speed and defense skills were remarkable. At just 19 years old, he was major league material.

SOME BASEBALL PLAYERS NEVER MAKE IT TO THE MAJORS, EVEN IF THEY'RE GOOD AT THE SPORT. TROUT'S TALENT HELPED HIM MOVE THROUGH MINOR LEAGUE BALL UNUSUALLY FAST.

MINOR LEAGUE BASEBALL CLASSES

LEVEL 1	ROOKIE TEAMS. THIS IS WHERE MOST PLAYERS START AFTER THEY'RE DRAFTED.
LEVEL 2	CLASS A SHORT SEASON
LEVEL 3	CLASS A (ALSO CALLED "LOW A")
LEVEL 4	CLASS A ADVANCED (ALSO CALLED "HIGH A")
LEVEL 5	DOUBLE A (AA)
LEVEL 6	TRIPLE A (AAA). THIS IS THE HIGHEST LEVEL OF MINOR LEAGUE BASEBALL. PLAYERS MOVE TO THE MAJORS FROM THIS LEVEL.

ROOKIE OF THE YEAR

In 2012, Trout made his MLB **debut** with the Los Angeles Angels. He **demonstrated** the same skills in the majors that he had in high school and in the minor leagues: power, strength, and **athleticism**.

Trout's talent for defense and high batting and scoring averages made for an awesome rookie year. Leading all the players in the American League, Trout had a .326 batting average. He hit 30 home runs and posted an impressive 83 RBIs. These spectacular stats made him the 2012 Rookie of the Year, and put him in the running for the American League's Most Valuable Player (MVP) award.

SPORTS CORNER

The Rookie of the Year award is given to the best rookie in Major League Baseball's American League and National League. Trout shared his honor with Bryce Harper of the Washington Nationals.

WHEN HE WAS NAMED ROOKIE OF THE YEAR, TROUT JOINED THE COMPANY OF BASEBALL GIANTS LIKE DEREK JETER, ALBERT PUJOLS, AND WILLIE MAYS.

BETTER AND BETTER

Trout followed up an amazing rookie year with an equally impressive second season. As a hitter, he recorded 109 runs and 110 walks, making his on-base percentage .432. His third season was great, too.

2014 MLB ALL-STAR GAME

2015 MLB ALL-STAR GAME

TROUT WON THE MLB ALL-STAR GAME MVP AWARD IN 2014 AND 2015. HE IS THE FIRST PLAYER TO EVER WIN THIS AWARD TWO YEARS IN A ROW.

In 2014, Trout helped the Angels finish with the best record in the American League, and the team made it to the playoffs. That same year, Trout was voted the American League MVP. He took home that award in both 2015 and 2016. As of 2017, Trout has earned a spot on the American League All-Star team every season since 2012.

ONE OF THE GREATS

As of 2017, Trout has been in the major leagues for five years. Experts and baseball lovers alike often say that Trout's first five years of baseball could be the greatest five-year career of all time.

If there were any doubts about that, Trout proved it true on his 26th birthday. On August 7, 2017, he made his 1,000th career hit. He joined other young baseball greats such as Ty Cobb, Mickey Mantel, and Hank Aaron, who reached this milestone by the age of 25. With stats like these, Trout is on his way to being one of the greatest baseball players in history!

SPORTS CORNER

In 2014, Trout signed a six-year contract with the Angels worth $144.5 million. When the contract expires, or runs out, in 2020, Trout will be a free agent.

TROUT'S LIST OF HONORS AND AWARDS CONTINUES TO GROW. TO DATE, HE HAS WON ROOKIE OF THE YEAR, AMERICAN LEAGUE MVP, SILVER SLUGGER, THE HANK AARON AWARD, AND THE ALL-STAR GAME MVP. HE'S EARNED A NUMBER OF THESE AWARDS MORE THAN ONCE!

THE FUTURE IS BRIGHT

It's always possible that professional athletes might get hurt while playing or practicing. In 2017, Trout hurt his thumb and had to have surgery. He couldn't play for a few weeks. Trout missed 39 games, which meant his 2017 stats were lower than past seasons.

But a setback like that couldn't stop Trout. Even though he missed time on the diamond, he still had 33 home runs, 72 RBIs, and led the league with an on-base percentage (OBP) of .442 in 2017. Trout's future is bright and this young athlete is sure to make history as one of baseball's greatest players.

GLOSSARY

athleticism: The qualities of athletes, such as strength, fitness, and being quick on their feet.

career: A period of time spent doing a job or activity.

debut: A first public appearance.

dedication: A feeling of very strong support for or loyalty to someone or something.

demonstrate: To show something clearly to other people.

draft: To choose someone to play on a professional sports team and the event when this takes place.

free agent: A sports player who is not under a contract and is therefore able to join any team they choose.

legend: A story coming down from the past that is popularly accepted but can't be checked; also a person who inspires legends.

professional: Having to do with a job someone does for a living.

prospect: Someone or something that is likely to succeed or to be chosen.

risk: Someone or something that may cause something bad or unpleasant to happen.

rookie: A first-year player in a professional sport.

scout: A person whose job it is to search for talented athletes.

CONTENTS

Aaron, Hank, 20
All-Star Game MVP, 19, 21
American League, 16, 19
American League MVP Award, 16, 19, 21

Cobb, Ty, 20

Doubleday, Abner, 4

Harper, Bryce, 16

Jeter, Derek, 17

Los Angeles Angels, 4, 12, 14, 16, 19, 20

Major League Baseball, 12, 16
Mantel, Mickey, 20
Mays, Willie, 17
Millville Senior High School, 8, 10

Pujols, Albert, 17

Rookie of the Year, 16, 17, 21

Silver Slugger, 21

Trout, Debbie, 6, 8
Trout, Jeff, 6, 7, 8

Washington Nationals, 16

WEBSITES

Due to the changing nature of Internet links, PowerKids Press has developed an online list of websites related to the subject of this book. This site is updated regularly. Please use this link to access the list: www.powerkidslinks.com/ysg/trout